Just for Two

A Collection of 5 Piano Duets in a Variety of Styles and Moods
Specially Written to Inspire, Motivate, and Entertain

DENNIS ALEXANDER

My *Just for You* piano solo collections were some of the first books that I wrote for Alfred Music Publishing Company. They have always been among the top sellers in my library. Now, I am delighted to share with you duet versions of many favorites from those solo books in my new series, *Just for Two*. Piano students always enjoy making music together. I hope that these duets will prove to be "twice the fun" of the original solo versions!

Enjoy, and happy music making.

Dennis Alexander

CONTENTS

Alfred Music Publishing Co., Inc.
P.O. Box 10003
Van Nuys, CA 91410-0003
alfred.com

ISBN-10: 0-7390-8801-7
ISBN-13: 978-0-7390-8801-2

ROLY-POLY RAG
Secondo

Dennis Alexander

ROLY-POLY RAG
Primo

Dennis Alexander

Secondo

Secondo

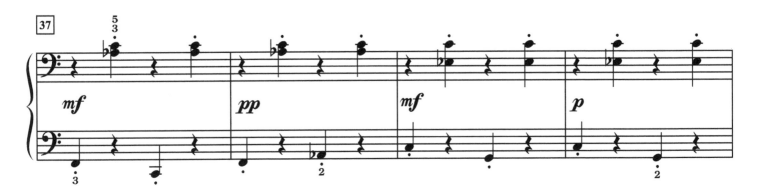

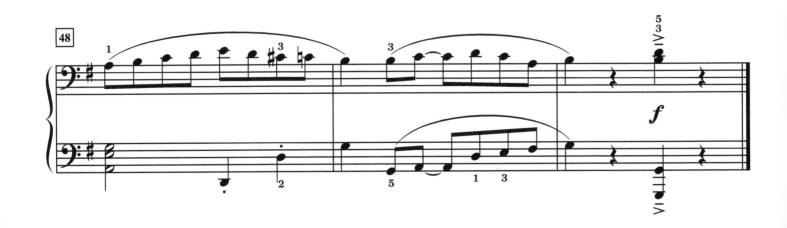

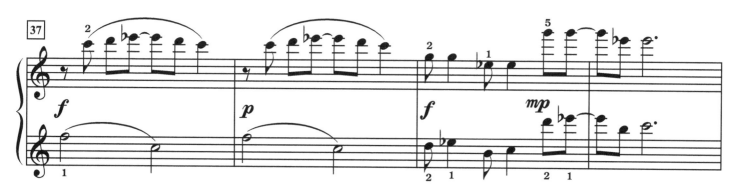

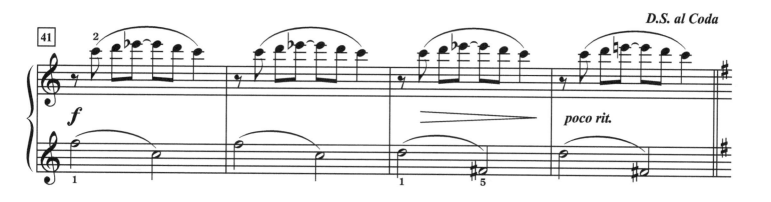

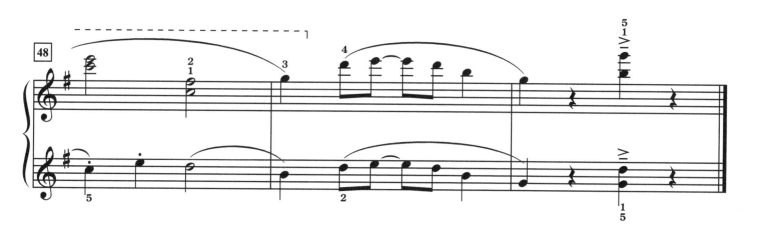

LULLABY FOR RYAN
Secondo

Dennis Alexander

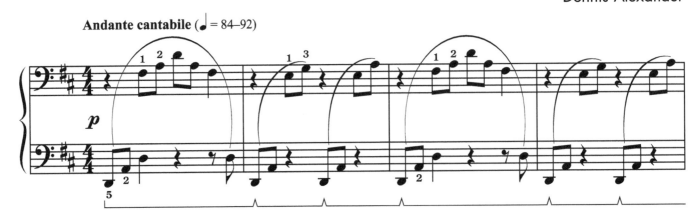

LULLABY FOR RYAN
Primo

Dennis Alexander

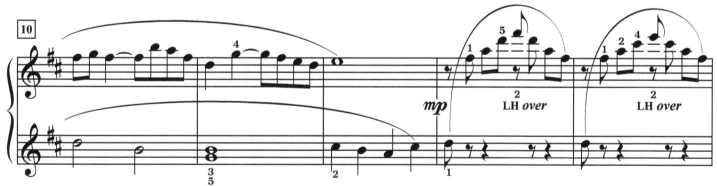

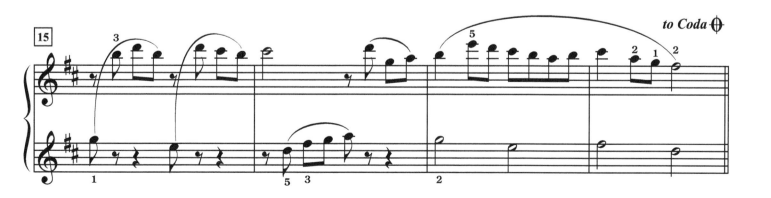

Secondo

COOL MOVE
Secondo

Dennis Alexander

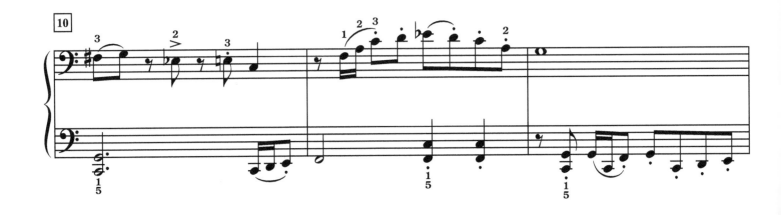

COOL MOVE
Primo

Dennis Alexander

Secondo

Secondo

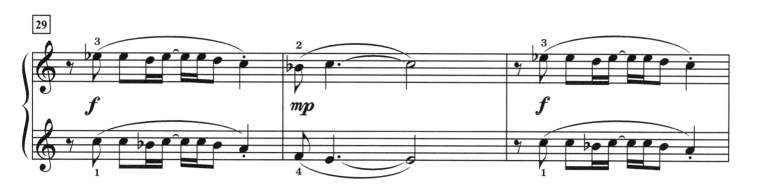

NOTTURNO IN E-FLAT MAJOR
Secondo

Dennis Alexander

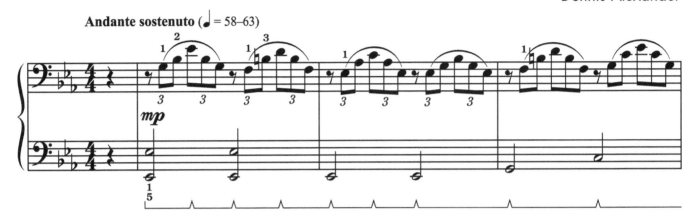

NOTTURNO IN E-FLAT MAJOR
Primo

Dennis Alexander

Secondo

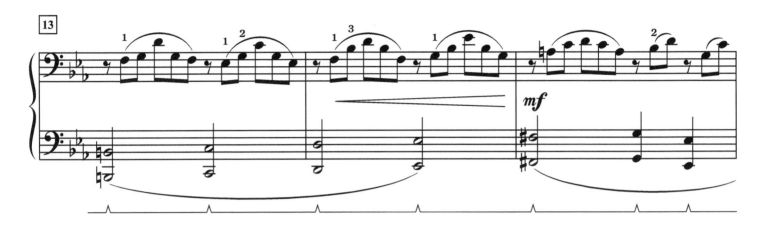

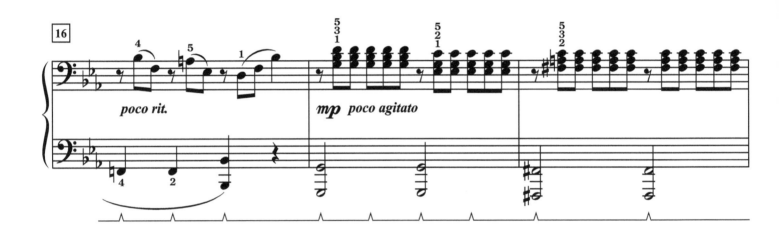

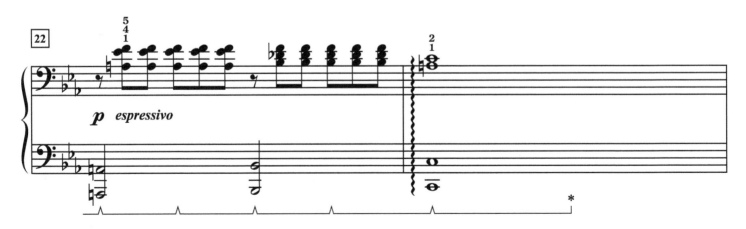

* Release the pedal on beat 3.

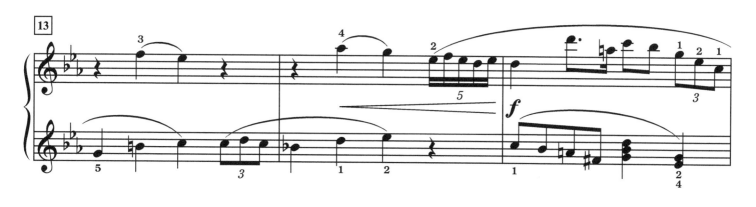

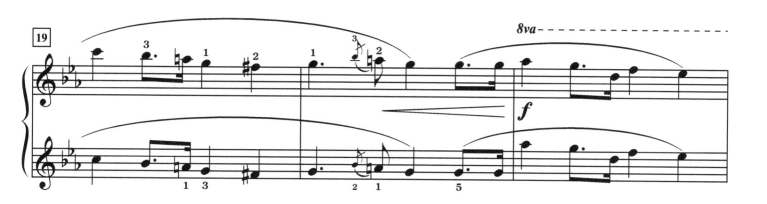

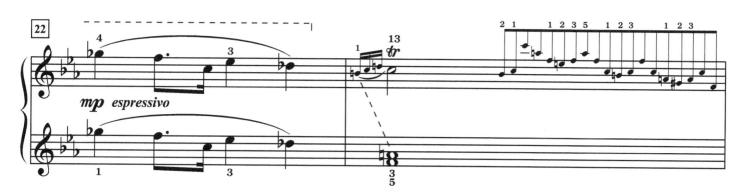

* Play the grace note slightly before the beat.

Secondo

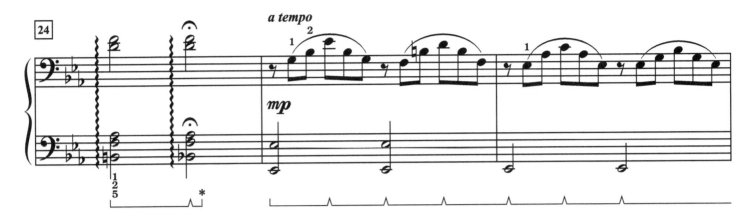

* Release the pedal when the primo begins the sixteenth notes.

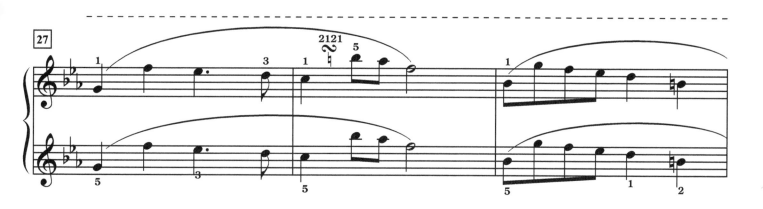

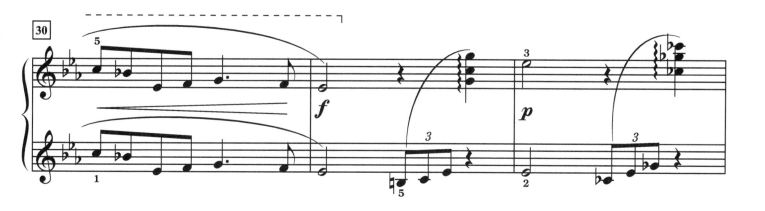

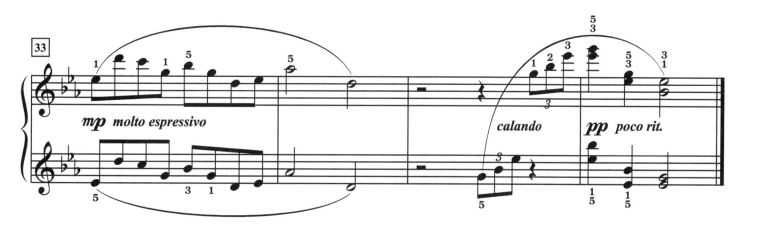

TARANTELLA FANTASTICO
Secondo

Dennis Alexander

TARANTELLA FANTASTICO
Primo

Dennis Alexander

26

Secondo

Secondo

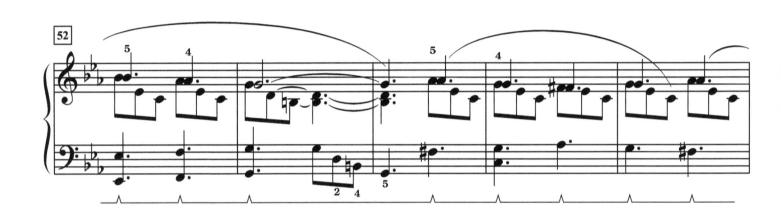

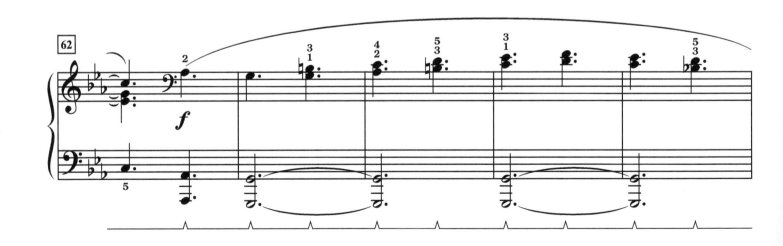

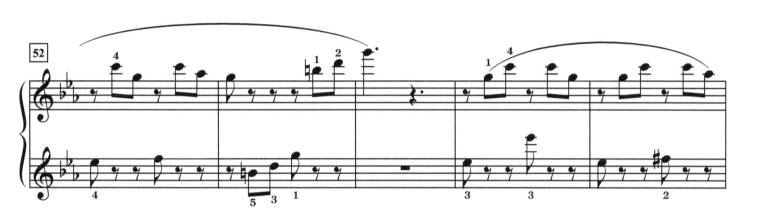

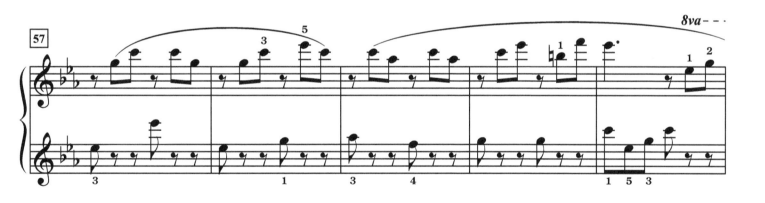

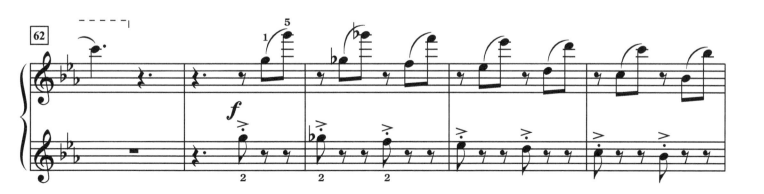

Secondo

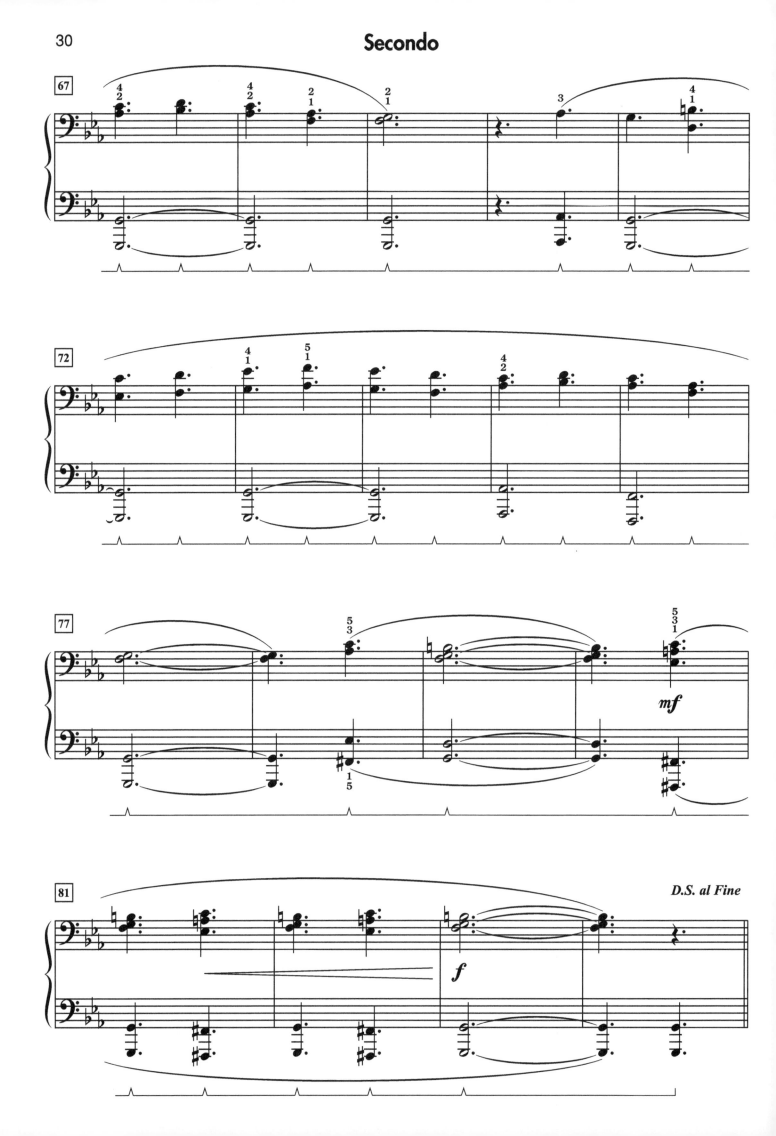